INCURABLY UNROMANTIC

For Camille
With love,
John
xx

INCURABLY UNROMANTIC

POEMS

John Gillies

Copyright © 2019 John Gillies

The moral right of the author has been asserted.

Apart from any fair dealing for the purposes of research or private study, or criticism or review, as permitted under the Copyright, Designs and Patents Act 1988, this publication may only be reproduced, stored or transmitted, in any form or by any means, with the prior permission in writing of the publishers, or in the case of reprographic reproduction in accordance with the terms of licences issued by the Copyright Licensing Agency. Enquiries concerning reproduction outside those terms should be sent to the publishers.

Matador
9 Priory Business Park,
Wistow Road, Kibworth Beauchamp,
Leicestershire. LE8 0RX
Tel: 0116 279 2299
Email: books@troubador.co.uk
Web: www.troubador.co.uk/matador
Twitter: @matadorbooks

ISBN 978 1789017 540

British Library Cataloguing in Publication Data.
A catalogue record for this book is available from the British Library.

Printed and bound in Great Britain by 4edge Limited
Typeset in 11pt Calibri by Troubador Publishing Ltd, Leicester, UK

Matador is an imprint of Troubador Publishing Ltd

For Annette,
who knows the real story

Contents

Advice to Heretics	1
Not Hard	2
Interring the Ashes	3
The Rough with the Smooth	4
Clearing Up	5
For the Defence	6
Writers' Panel	7
Betjemania	9
Mr. Larkin is on Facebook	10
Body-snatching	11
Incurably Unromantic	12
Self-Evaluations or Carpy Diem	13
Oresteia	14
Guilt or Alice in Pizzaland	15
In the Stockyards of the Stars	17
The Men in Dark Blue Suits	18
Where the Desert Begins	19

Taking No Chances	20
Cat	21
A Revised Estimate	22
Out On The Lawn	23
Two Major Faults	24
Graffiti	25
Permanent Revolution	28
Punta Arenas	30
The Palestine Campaign	31
A Moscow Cabbie Speaks	33
The Sticking Place	34
A True Tale	36
The Ecological Question – and the Answer	37
The Darker Part	40
You	41
Cabo Girâo	42
Stop and Search	43
Country Music	44
Beside the Point	45
Not again	46

Come-uppance	47
Groot Begijnhof, Leuven	48
26 . 02	49
"Specific Exclusions: (i) High Risk Sports …	50
Playing the Maze Game	51
Bread and Butter Pudding	52
A Slate Tombstone	53
Love Song	55
A Shock Result in the National Ploughing Championships	56
Did Jesus Snore?	57

Advice to Heretics

When the Grand Inquisitor
Is your next visitor
And he asks if you've something to say –
If you can't Torquemada
The whole enchilada
It's best to keep auto-da-fé.

Not Hard

"Once coffins were substantial – hand-carved oak,
With full brass fittings. This thing's just a joke,"
I told the undertaker. "Plywood, cheap
Veneer – and plastic handles! I won't sleep
At night if my Dad's laid to his last rest
In joinerwork that would disgrace a chest
Of drawers a blind man wouldn't buy."

The undertaker sighed a patient sigh.
"The casket, sir, has been designed to burn.
Most folk prefer to spend more on the urn –
("to spend more than they earn?")
That's what contains
What, after all, remains of the – remains.
Light-weight construction. swift initiation
Of more efficient, full incineration.
Low density materials. High combustible mass."

So, Dad, it's cardboard oak and plastic brass –
Cheap, functional, light-weight and purpose-built –
Not hard to bear – the burden of this gilt.

Interring the Ashes

And so it came to pass, three atheists
And one not-absolutely-lapsed RC
Stood with heads bowed in Presbyterian prayer
Over a varnished box, eight inches square –
Smaller than the shoe-box, it occurred to me,
In which we buried Jake the hamster
In a grave no shallower than this,
Dug with more care
And infinitely greater reverence. Love consists
In tiny deeds against the grain of life:
The almost-Catholic hugged his atheist wife
And whispered his line on cue, "We must be brave."

The sun glared sullenly between the pylons. There
The matter rested. Three shovelfuls of earth
Removed and two replaced. I turned to slip
The wet-nosed gravedigger a ten pound tip –
"Two quid a shovelful," I thought, but it was worth
That much, and more, to feel a momentary
Connection to the eternal arbitrary
Schema that constrained us. When I tripped
Over the spade, that, too, was in the script.

The Rough with the Smooth

The Old Man would have choked with spleen
If he had thought that one day I would tip
An Irishman ten quid for shovelling grit
On to his coffin – But he would have been
Considerably mollified, I'm sure, to see
This lovely view he has of the distillery.

Clearing Up

Ripping black bin-bags from a roll, I wonder vaguely
How many will be needed. Some of his jackets
Are in quite good condition – nearly new, in fact.
The white cap with the Bowling Club insignia
Still in its plastic cover. Best to wrap
The photographs in sweaters for protection.
A hairbrush and a comb, and – curiously –
His bottom denture only. Birthday cards
From Helen and from me. A large-print book
(John Creasey) – doubtless never read. His diary
A catalogue of "Quiet days", relieved
By "Pension day" or "Paid the Council Tax"
Or "Home help called". A lop-eared china dog
Tilts its head inquiringly. It begins to seem
As if four bags may, after all, have been
An over-estimate.

For the Defence

"We've lost the art of ritual, the sense
Of how to formalise emotion – take
The funeral service – there's a case in point:
Action and emotion out of joint –
No channel for our feelings, more a defence
Against them. The old-fashioned wake
Allowed for grieving on a human scale –
Now it's taped organ music and a few stale
Words, then close the velvet drape –
Literally and figuratively, there's no shape,
No outline, no Gestalt to make us feel
That what we've just experienced was real –"

He paused and took a sip of his Chablis –
And that was when I hit him. Well, you see,
I felt somebody had to take a stand
In favour of the gutless and the bland.
The only time I really get enraged
Is when some bastard knocks the unengaged –
Alienation? Anomie?
Angst and Weltschmerz? That's for me!

Writers' Panel

"Impossible to say – I really can't
Recall a time I wasn't writing. Mum
Still has the exercise books with the extant
Scribblings – my little stories, poems, some
Character sketches – all of the too-clever-
By-two-thirds detritus of whatever
Precedes one's juvenilia –
Infantilia?"

Me next. Can I admit how *easily*
I can recall a time – a thousand times –
I wasn't writing – when any measly
Excuse was good enough: the rhymes
Just wouldn't come, or came too glibly –
The sky too blue, the Ginger Nuts too nibbly –
Reactance against being lectured, sermoned:
Skiving, like neurosis, is over-determined.
Where would Adonais be if Shelley
Had owned a telly?
Where would his Mistresse be if Donne
Had taken five to catch the News at Onne
And realised, too late, that he'd sat through

"Neighbours", "The Oprah Show" Parts One and Two
(This week – "Women Who Beat Their Husbands") –

"Same here, really – I suppose one day
They'll isolate that strip of DNA
That codes the writing mania – In future years,
Geneticists and Bioengineers
Will offer us a cure, or will at least
Offer our mothers early terminations
Before they have to bring forth such a beast –
Driven to populate the imaginations
Of innocent folks with monsters from the Id.
It's a compulsion – no point trying to kid
Ourselves – Writing is rape, and chemical castration
By means of alcohol the only certain
Way to keep the public safe. As Richard Burton
Remarks in The Anatomy of Melancholy,
Writers drink, not from self-destructive folly
But as a higher form of public service –

Sorry about all this crap – I'm really nervous!"

Betjemania

When I am dead, let me be laid
Beside Clarecastle station,
Where kind hearts know
No quid pro quo,
And love no alteration.

Above the tracks, the footbridge backs,
Gull-winged, on thermal rises;
The sunlight crawls
Along the walls
Where Guinness advertises,

And curious ramblers turn the rusted lock,
Consult the faded timetable, the shattered clock,
And walk the sleepers – lest the Sleepers walk.

Mr. Larkin is on Facebook

My virtual friends update their status daily,
Their virtual tags deface each other's walls
Like wandering dogs —"Pissed here today in passing,
Barked at a child, lay down and licked my balls..."

Or village dogs in a sierra night-time
One sets the others off —"I'm here!" — "I'm over here!"
As if the volume of their pointless barking
Would make the point of their existence clear.

We shouldn't, I suppose, be too dismissive —
Perhaps the self-same impulse gives us art
As prompts the schoolboy's small self-affirmation
To impress his fellows with the loudest fart.

We couldn't all, I guess, be Bach or Shakespeare
But our rage against the dying of the light
Still drives us to proclaim ourselves to others.
It's just a pity most of it is shite.

Body-snatching

"Why dig that up again?" you said,
As if I'd tried to resurrect the dead.
But, in our partnership, I wouldn't care
To say which one is Burke and which is Hare.

I'd say that I was truer to the part
Because, like them, I lack the steely heart
And find that, usually, I must get pissed
Before I can turn Resurrectionist –

You, my dear Doctor Knox, coolly despise
Wretches who bring you corpses to anatomise.

Incurably Unromantic

"You Social Psychologists have got your work cut out
To try to rationalise what Love is all about –
'Need-Complementarity, Secondary Reinforcement,
Social Comparison, Central Value Endorsement,
Cognitive Balance, Congruence, Asset-matching' –
It's more than mutual back (and belly) scratching:
It's marvellous, mysterious, mischievous, misguided –
A myriad, multifarious, many-sided
Mystery, too deep for tears or wishing – !"

"I see," I said, "you don't share my ambition
To roam the woods and hear the sweet dove sing:
'Post-decisional Dissonance Reduction
is a Many Splendour'd Thing!"

Self-Evaluations or Carpy Diem

"Now I'm the sort of person who –"
(Most often said, I find, least often true)
"Takes others at their own evaluation,
And can't fight the temptation
To put my trust in places where it's liable
To be stamped on. I realise the Bible
Is on my side, but you would really think
That I would finally get wise – would sink
Into the cynicism others display
For self-defence – but, as I say,
I can't mistrust – a sap, a True Believer!"

My fingers found the handle of the cleaver
And closed around it – though I'd no intention
Of doing more than testing his contention.

Oresteia

"Clytaemnestra, where are you ?
Agamemnon's back! Yoo hoo!
Hubby's home! – You, where's my wife?"

"Maybe in bed, sire. How can I
Put this to you? On my life,
You wouldn't have me tell a lie ..
Clytaemnestra's not your wife –
Not in the eyes of Zeus. I fear
I'm not making this too clear –
To come right out, she's now the mistress
Of your own cousin, Lord Aegisthus.
I – uh – wouldn't go in there, if I were you ..."

Guilt or Alice in Pizzaland

I saw this book called "Guilt: How to Let Go" –
Subtitle, "Kicking the Guilt Trip" – Well, you know
Me – bought the thing, then, right away
Felt *really* guilty – well, I mean to say,
Twelve ninety-five for a book! How was I gonny
Tell Brian? It's no' as if he's really fondy
Post-Bernean self-analysis – or spendin' money –
I mind o' askin' him wance – jist tae be funny –
"Brian, whit dae you say after you say Hello?"
He mulls it over for a minute – "Ah don't know –
Nuthin' –" Well, that wis right – Ten outy ten –
So then, when he starts moanin' –
"*Whit,* fish cakes *again*?"
Ah says, "I'm savin' up tae get EST."
"Electric shocks?" he says, "Ah thought they were free
On the National Health!" – "Naw, Erhard Seminars Trainin' –
They lock ye up and shout at ye a' day –

                                      ferr does yer brain in!"
"Sounds jist like bein' merrit – Zur nae HP sauce?" –

Well, when I say No, I feel guilty – it's the loss
Of self-esteem, the sense of having failed
To meet a self-set standard – self-impaled
On a self-made dilemma I, in fact, reject –
"Fish cakes an' nae sauce! Wherr's yer self-respect?"
Well, that was it. I snapped. My case is still tae
Come up before the Sheriff – but I'm pleadin' Guilty!"

In the Stockyards of the Stars

In the stockyards of the stars,
they shave the comet's hair
prior to execution. The aurora
shrieks in the darkness. Behind bars,
asteroids mill. The air
freezes their breath.
On the event horizon
hangs the unmade instant of their death.

Luncheon-meat sandwiches in Tupperware.
Brown's Bay Primary. A pool of piss.
Chalk dust in sunshafts. Pallid blue
walls that echo Mr. Rees's stare –
"I really doubt if we can find a pair
of clean shorts for a boy as big as you" –
On the event horizon
only this.
Crush down the tears that menace
everything.

The Men in Dark Blue Suits

The Men in Dark Blue Suits all keep their eyes
on their notes as, one by one, they take their turn
to roll the silence flat with their smooth voices,
back and forth, leaving the grassy surface
striped in contrasting diagonals; their ties
echo the pattern perfectly.
Hypocrisy hangs heavy on their hands –
time so light it must be tethered to
the table-top, lest it should fly.
On plastic silver salvers, sandwiches
languish unloved. The percolator
strains and, with a gasp, brings forth
a tiny puke of fluid. We've done well
to heed their previous advice; the feedback
has improved beyond all expectation.
A blue-suited fly conducts
a thorough quality review
of the remaining tuna and tomato
sandwiches.

Where the Desert Begins

What shall we do when we reach the place
Where the desert begins?
What if we should lose one another
Or turn back, defeated?
Where the road markings end and then
The road itself, the mind's eye
Pearls into blindness.
A hundred horizons merge, directionless –
Yet strike out we must
In search of something we can't even picture.

Time enough to worry about all that, you reckon?
I expect you're right – I always meet
Trouble three quarter-way – just like my Dad,
"Aye lookin' for snaw an' there's nane fa'in'..."

Taking No Chances

In the springtime darkness, Dad's torch dazzles
The dahlias. Moving from bloom to bloom,
He delicately picks up the earwigs
In his own giant pincers, thumb and forefinger,
Whose tips are blackened with the juice
Of their crushed corpses. He works in silence
Lest his breathing should alert the enemy.
They are called earwigs, after all – Who knows
If they're stone deaf or hyperacusic? –
Anything's possible.

Cat

Blacker than her own shadow, she drifts
across the silvered surface of the room.
Behind her, the lamplight smoothes its hair
carefully back in place. Evening arrives,
riding the sudden rain. The chair
receives her silently – divides and sifts
her darkness from its own. The green eyes close
and, once again, she's handed over
to us – her temporary nominees –
the custody of that closed realm which she's
assigned to guard. Dreams, like a breeze,
ripple her back and tickle at her nose.

A Revised Estimate

Deep in the bone, the marrow seethes.
The pain's excruciating – "But at least
it shows there's something going on," we say.
"Her breathing's easier already." Play
familiar games in unfamiliar ways.

"It's a large dose – not really massive – but
enough to shrink the secondaries in the gut.
I'm afraid, although we can't say with precision,
our estimate may need downward revision."

The visit to Siena? Ally's baby?
Dinner at Devonshire's? – That's still a maybe.

Out On The Lawn

(after W.H.Auden)
(after 7 lagers and a curry)

Out on the lawn I lie in bed,
Vague ache and sick hue, unsober head –
And the wine last night's off-tune.
Furry stuffs green my tongue complete –
The day's sick livery.
My feet
Point to the rice and moong.

Two Major Faults

Last night we played a brand new game –
"Two Major Faults" – and when it came
Your turn, you called me pedant and
Irremediably bland.
Though I said "Thank you for that gift!"
I won't pretend I wasn't miffed –
Given that your only faults
Are skin that sparkles and a taste for salt.

Graffiti

In the underpass, leading to the railway station
(or from the station,
depending on your destination
and orientation),
they've tried out a new tactic –
a prophylactic,
a pre-emptive strike
against graffiti artists and the like:
Instead of leaving bare, inviting wall,
they've filled it all
with faux-naif but tasteful daubs
of toning browns and ochres – blobs
that, when you view
them through
half-closed or just myopic eyes
resolve themselves (surprise, surprise)
into the shapes of trains – a railroad theme!
A locomotive leitmotiv – quel crafty scheme!

Dark and disorderly, the constant shift
of shape and texture as they drift,
leaves no extended space,
no open, unclaimed place
for Pentel vandal to deface —
Yet, into each
available niche,
each tiny nook,
just look —
some Nicholas Hilliard
of the billiard hall —
some master miniature
painter's signature
is squeezed — and all
you need (or want) to know:
who loves whom, who's a slag, and where to go
for good cock-fun is etched in 9-point microscript,
patiently crafted in this heart-felt-tipped
efflorescence of self-affirmation.

Now, any primitive can subjugate
blank wall, white canvas, virgin litho-plate –
Real art arises in the interplay
of mind and medium, *"surface et pensée"* –

Just as in Altamira or Lascaux,
a lump or bump or hump was no
dissuasion –
but rather the *occasion*
for bison's swelling shoulder, stag's curved rump –
that which impedes
only succeeds
in giving form to all our unformed needs.
Here in this concrete cavern, new cave artists
send the old message – "We're still here, you bastards!"

Permanent Revolution

In the cemetery, organised resistance
must, of necessity, be underground –
Communication's hampered by the distance
from lair to lair – and even infrasound
is muffled by wet clay. Raising the spirits
of those too long downtrodden is, at best
of times, a Herculean task, but here it's
positively superhuman – "Let us rest!"

It's no surprise, since being alive and dying
are wholly individualistic acts,
to find the newly dead at first denying
the simple yet-to-be-acknowledged fact
that being dead's the only true collective
form of action. Each one's basic aim –
to beat the rap on Judgement Day's effective
for all – a classical zero-sum game.

In life, they won only at the expense of others'
losses: in death, however, all can win
if only they unite – sisters and brothers
beneath the shroud, if not beneath the skin.

And now, before the Judge at the Last Battle
their spokesman says – "I'd like to read a list
of our demands!", while Heaven fills with the rattle
of a million upraised, skeletal clenched fists –

Death, after all, is only temp'ry –
"Hasta la victoria siempre!"

Punta Arenas

Driving to meet you at the airport, I recall
the expedition that set out from Punta Arenas
and headed south, drawn on a thread of sound –
the thousand-mile-distant groaning of the ice.
Their mission: to capture *"un iceberg"* (no word
exists in Spanish, strangely) – and to tow it
the length of the Atlantic to Seville –
the centrepiece of Chile's contribution
to Expo '92. My expedition's
no less ambitious. Will you melt before
we reach the contraflow at Junction Twelve?

The Palestine Campaign

The young man from the agency chewed his pencil –
"What you need, Mr. Pilate – or can I call you Pontius? –
is a fresh market profile. These are image- conscious
times and Judea – let's face it 's – not exactly Trendsville.

The Roman Empire – OK – strong corporate identity –
established house-style: eagles, triumphal arches,
crucified slaves and gladiators – but Macho's
no longer in – not really, well, First Century.

The new campaign will focus on the caring
face of Pax Romana – so we're talking meek –
the power of gentleness, the other cheek –
Pontius, in one word, we are talking *sharing.*

We open on a tracking shot across
a sea of upturned faces – Hebrew zealots –
(soft but expectant music – possibly Vangelis) –
A team of soldiers with a wooden cross –

and then the camera tilts up to show – yourself
up on the balcony – a quizzical frown,
compassionate and troubled – gazing down
upon the silent mob below – a wealth

of meaning in that look – "This man abhors
all violence," it says. We hold it for
a full five seconds as the music fades –
then straight into your speech – don't fret, the lot
will be held up on cue-cards, out of shot.
It's not quite finished but, in effect, it trades

the preacher for the murderer – a stroke
of brilliance by our writers! – then a storm
of cheers. Voice-over: "A milestone in penal reform!"
You wave – just once – then re-adjust your cloak

and turn to shake the preacher's hand. You toss him
a nod, a quiet smile – not too upbeat –
A simple human moment – brothers meet.
Freeze-frame. Now is that mega-chills – or merely awesome?

A Moscow Cabbie Speaks

When eventually it emerged that Socialism
Had, after all, only been Stalinism
And the Beloved Leader
Was a nasty little bleeder,
A few of us began to wonder
What other little blunder
Might come to light
Before the Party finally got it right.
Eurocommunism turned out to be
Social Democracy –
Your British Labour Party
Was the SDP –
And your King Arthur, seemingly, was King Canute,
And paid his mortgage with Ghaddafi's loot –
And the Bucharest People's Militia's first job
Was to rescue
Ceaucescu
From the Bucharest mob.

Now, cynicism is cheap, that's understood –
But I'm idealist enough still to believe
That just 'cos a thing's cheap don't mean it's no good –
Sorry, I don't take roubles – Euros or dollars, please.

The Sticking Place

The bumper sticker caught my eye –
"Life's a Bitch – Then You Die!"
"Well," I thought, "it makes a change
From *'Windsurfers Do It Standing Up'* –
'My other car's a Porsche!'..." – the strange
Thing was the nodding Snoopy pup
On the back shelf: it didn't quite add up –
Schulz and Schopenhauer in a middle-range
Fiesta 1.3 – "Happiness Is
A Nihilistic Aphorism"? – His
And Hers, perhaps? – Male dark
And female light – Ahuramazda
Reborn here in the car park
Outside Asda?
Thanatos and Eros? Ying and Yang?
The female Steady State, the male Big Bang?

'We've Seen the Lions Of Longleat'
- I've seen the Angel of Death.
'Rugby Players Have Oval Balls'
- But they end up out of breath.
'Keepa Da Hands Off – Mafia Staff Car'
- Impersonal menace: a hint of Kafka.
'Sex Lessons: For Details, Please Apply
To Driver' – but Love lessens too, and dies.
'This Car Has Constipation – It Hasn't Passed
A Thing for Weeks', etcetera – until at last
Over his epitaph, his loved ones weep:
'Please Pass Quietly – Driver Asleep'.

A True Tale

He said —
"A tank crew on manoeuvres sold
Their vehicle to a country tavern-keeper
For two cases of vodka and some cold
Sausage — They refused to sell it cheaper.

Mine host disposed of it a.s.a.p.
To a pair of shrewd scrap-metal dealers.
When finally traced, it had turned into three
Hundred and nine gross of potato-peelers."

"As tall a story as I've heard, old chap!"
I said, "As if these folks would risk their necks!"
Until he told me the whole bunch — the scrap-
dealers, innkeeper and troops were Czechs.

The Ecological Question – and the Answer

Before the human race goes down
For the third and final time, to drown
In a tideless sea
Of garbage, we
May perhaps muse pensively –
Given that we knew
What we ought to do,
How was it that we came to screw
Things up so comprehensively?

Did the Naked Ape
Just get too big for his boots?
Or does the planet's rape
Have deeper roots?

Was it pie-in-the-sky
Religions that led us
To cast a cold eye
On the mother that fed us –
The millenarian
Heresy – or was it loss

Of spirituality that cost
The earth — Utilitarian
Proto-economistic attitudes
That drowned us in plastic and in platitudes?

Was it capitalism
And exploitation,
Materialism
And alienation?
Or was the problem emotion
And blind devotion
In place of rationality?
Was the problem men
And androgen
And territoriality?
Was it Bible-ism
Linked to tribalism —
Too much faith and not much charity?
The great, illogical
Lure of dreams —
Of ideological
Football teams?

Are even environmentalists
Fundamentally fundamentalists?

It's a sad reflection
On introspection
That the answer's so easy to see –
Would this ghastly, absurd
Mess ever have occurred,
If people were just – well – more like me?

The Darker Part

Behind the drowning clematis, the wall's
Still hopeful of a breakthrough. Time and distance
Bicker in corners. Stone laps crumbling stone,
Like sleepy cats who indiscriminately
Lick self and other. Always there's a moment
In any garden, when I look your way
And sense your sudden longing for the earth –
The darker part – the stone in the stream's bed –
Nights without stars.

You

You're the cream in my coffee
You're the salt in my wound
You're the bullet lodged near my heart
That makes breathing a wee bit difficult at times

Cabo Girâo

Gonçalves Zarco, thinking he had reached
the western limit of this coast and world,
turned back towards Funchal, naming the place
Cape Turnaround – and, when a second voyage
revealed his error, let the name remain.
Beneath the eucalyptus, every flower's
a candidate for CITES listing. Lizards
cling to the cliff, indifferent to the facts.
A falcon pauses, measuring the distance.
The tourist guide ushers her charges back
towards the coach. The lady from Dumfries
is unimpressed – the second highest sea-
cliff in the world doesn't look like much
from where she's standing. Captain Zarco might
have felt his judgement vindicated – After all,
a Viewing Point is only a point of view.

Stop and Search

Mind-blocks have been set up, mature trees felled
across each major highway, country road
and bridle-path that leads to memory.
                                    Armed volunteers
execute their instructions ruthlessly –
a text-book operation.
                                    But, meanwhile,
abandoning your vehicle, you've slipped
across the unploughed fields and through the woods –
cut all the trip-wires, drugged the prowling dogs,
cracked all the access codes and here you are,
relaxing in my chair and leafing casually
through your own dossier.

Country Music

Well, I tried to call you from the mall like we'd arranged –
But each time I'd try, no reply – seemed kind of strange.
So I drove on over to discover if you were OK,
And I tried to think of all the things that I wanted to say –

  But my mind went blank and my heart sank thru the floor
  When I saw his pick-up parked outside your door.

Thought of all those times when your line had been engaged –
How you wouldn't speak for a week when you got enraged –
And those tire-tracks at the back of the shack last fall –
It made perfect sense – I was dense not to see it all –

  But my mind went blank and my heart sank thru the floor
  When I saw his pick-up parked outside your door.

Now I beg you, Judge, don't begrudge me my last say –
My defense don't make sense, but I'll tell you anyway –
Don't remember I dismembered Mary Belle –
Can't recollect how I dissected him as well

  'Cos my mind went blank and my heart sank thru the floor
  When I saw his pick-up parked outside her door.

Beside the Point

"The wind is the darling whore of the sea,"
I had translated carefully.
Miss Mosen frowned: "That won't quite do.
You can't say that. 'Buhldirne' , it is true,
Means – what you said – but that's beside
The point. I am the Editor and I decide
What can go into the school magazines.
'Sweetheart' is more acceptable and means
Much the same thing."

                     If she were here now, I'd ask her
If that's why my relationships are such disasters.

Not again

On Hatfield Road, my fingers move
Automatically to the indicator switch — left turn
Into your street. Again I find myself
In the wrong lane, wrong traffic stream,
Wrong year. How long, I ask myself,
Is the half-life of a habit?
A hire-drive Escort van waves me back
Out into the flow. Only a couple of minutes
Wasted this time. Could have been worse.

Come-uppance

Puffed up with his own self-impotence, he thinks
The sky's his oyster. Constantly barking up
The wrong end of the stick, he shows
His true colours to the mast – but never quite manages
To hit the hammer on the head. His problem is
He wants to have his cake both ways –
Live dangerously, burn the midnight oil
At both ends, but always have a safety-net
Hanging over him.

                       One of these days his chickens
Will come home to roast before they're hatched –
But, until then, why should I care? I mean to say,
It's no skin off *my* teeth – As far as I'm concerned,
It's a case of half of one
And six dozen of the other.

Groot Begijnhof, Leuven

The lank brown river slides with little grace
Between the stucco and the black-baked walls –
Traces a scar across the face
Of Albertspark, until it falls
Under the mill-wheel. By St. Michael's gate,
A sycamore in bud recalls
The never-answered need to contemplate
Without anticipation – the same hand holds
Two dozen threads – one perfect square of lace.

26 . 02

Some moments borrow their intensity
from half- or mis-remembered gestures.
Cosmopolitan's "Star Guide to your Sex Life" –
"Gemini – Hot Date: the twenty-sixth of February.
Erogenous Zone: back of the knee."
                                              Here goes.
Today's the day and, frankly, things
have reached the point of quiet desperation.

"Specific Exclusions: (i) High Risk Sports …

e.g. playing with a Political Football
in a Political Minefield, where the Opposition
keeps Moving the Goalposts …. "

Playing the Maze Game

I say, "You don't understand…"
I mean, "You understand too well."
You say, "You're right, I don't…"
You mean, "You're wrong, I do."

Each watching our virtual whiteboards,
Trying
To form meta-maps of the other's semantic space,
Grasping for heuristics that might represent
Some kind of Shared Reality in an incomplete,
Bog-basic, two-dimensioned, single-surface kind of way,
We play
The Maze Game – "Interpersonal Exploration for
The Cartographically Challenged
(Not Suitable for the Under-Sevens)".

Bread and Butter Pudding

(after Tacitus)

They made a piece
And they called it dessert.

A Slate Tombstone

> *Sacred to the memory of*
> *Grace Inch*
> *beloved wife of John Murray,*
> *Slater in Biggar,*
> *who died September 11th, 1870*
> *aged 26 years*

A pillar of plum-purple slate among
the wind-blurred sandstones, lichened granites,
its hundred year history has left it cold:
the serifs still hard as a cry, bevels unsoftened –
the winter light still cuts as deep
into her name and his. He knew his slate all right –
saw how it might be worked and heavy-honed –
and how, even on this hilltop where the poplars fail
to hold the driven rain, it could
stand like a lance against the day and dark.
In that place where memories weather
to comforting softness,
details drown in overgrowth of grey irrelevance,
this ruthlessly remains.

All this he willed – yet overlooked
how granite and sandstone fall in grains like time;
slate's layered like memory.
The rain has left no scar but ran its nails,
probing in parallel, along the flank until,
one autumn morning or biting winter night,
the column cracked like fire.
Some memories abrade, some overgrow –
he saw that right –
but there's another enemy that infiltrates
invisibly until the first hard frost
opens the structure in a single cut.

Somebody, vaguely moved to do the right thing,
has propped the fractured cross against the plinth.

Love Song

Sometimes all I need is the air that I breathe
And to love you ....
Other times I need pizza.

A Shock Result in the National Ploughing Championships

"He's a Kilkenny man — I'm sure of that!"
Says Higson, broaching his pint in Tulley's —
His moustache drawing fine furrows
In the sweet grey foam —
"A big-arsed bastard too."
                                      Outside, in Tullow Street,
The twilight's just beginning to get up steam.
"Never seen him before — not once," says somebody.
"Bloody strange thing," Higson insists,
patting his pockets till he hears
the comforting rattle of his box of Swans,
"coming to Carlow just the once
and winning the damn thing."
                "Was there not another case
back in the Fifties?" Tommy Forgan says.
"The Fifties!" — Higson spits towards the fire
and watches the gobbet sizzle on the grate.

Did Jesus Snore?

Did Jesus snore?
He ate and drank –
He'd have a crap,
But not a wank?

He was a man
Who never sinned –
But did he scratch?
Did he break wind?

He was divine
Yet wholly human –
So was he turned on
By a woman?

To be like us
He must have known
Some stirrings in
The nether zone.

Some days did he
Feel less than chummy
Because of piles
Or a dodgy tummy?

We hear that he
Felt human pains,
But which? And where?
No-one explains.

Great Caesar – he
Was epileptic –
The boils on Marx's
Bum turned septic

Pope Leo the Tenth
Had hammer toes
(The same as me)
And so it goes –
Particular men
Have their diseases –
But *which* did God
Inflict on Jesus?

You can't just say "It's a divine mystery
How God decided his medical history..."
Did he catch any major childhood diseases?
Or even occasional coughs and sneezes?
A touch of Glue Ear? Or a hint of a squint
(which, later in life, he would happily lose)?
Did he never go through the "Terrible Twos"?
Even as a child, was his natural piety
Such as to spare Mum one moment's anxiety?

If all this is so, then I ask you flat –
What kind of "fully human" is that?